THE ALCHEMY OF REIKI

OPENING THE DOOR TO ENERGY WORK

LINDA MCCANN

Copyright © 2018 Linda McCann

All Rights Reserved
No part of this publication may be reproduced
in any form, without written permission
from the author.

ISBN13: 978-1724468857
Printed in the United States of America

I would like to dedicate this book to my family and students.
Without you the book wouldn't have been possible.
Thanks for your support!

CONTENTS

Chapter 1:	Introduction	1
Chapter 2:	Reiki	11
Chapter 3:	The Reiki Treatment	28
Chapter 4:	The Energy Body	33
Chapter 5:	Chakras	37
Chapter 6:	Dowsing	42
Chapter 7:	Attunements	67
Chapter 8:	Reiki II	70
Chapter 9:	Cho Ku Rei	73
Chapter 10:	Sei Hei Ki	77
Chapter 11:	Hon Sha Ze Sho Nen	80
Chapter 12:	Guardian Angels	85

A Complete Reiki Treatment
Disclaimer Notice
Dowsing Chart
The Reiki Ideals

Historically, Alchemy was a singular practice although an apprentice may have been acquired if the Alchemist needed the assistance and felt the need to share knowledge. The job of the Alchemist (Scientist) was to try to understand matter/energy and the building blocks of the world. Experiments and the keeping of a written journal allowed the Alchemist to build on an insight into vast knowledge. Some may have been searching for the formula to transmute lead into gold. Imagine that! If that knowledge has ever been found I for one don't know anything about it. The formulae became an important tool, especially as written down for the Alchemist to help others if so inclined and to teach. Everything is comprised of energy. The Alchemist was searching for a way to harness and use the possibility of a vast amount of power at his disposal if he could only find the right formulae.

Your personal journey to learn about energy, how it works and how you can integrate it into your life for a variety of uses is the reason that you are reading this today. We will learn Reiki, some of the applications and how to **transmute** by adding modalities, utilizing intention and focusing which becomes a form of Alchemy. Alchemy was intended to create a formula by changing certain elements into something other and that is what you will be doing when you learn and use all these tools. Alchemists were a combination of Scientist and spiritual seeker. I have always been fascinated by Alchemy and have made a limited study of its history. You will be "changing" the way you think and interact on an energetic level. The journey will bring you to a deeper understanding of yourself and the world you are a part of. Alchemy in Reiki uses specific formulas which the practitioner develops for themselves by writing down and remembering what works and what doesn't. Alchemy for you as the practitioner will also become part of your Shamanistic way of thinking and viewing your world and your work. The transformation or alchemical reaction may not be visible to the naked eye, however a change is effected at some level. By combining the energy along with other gifts, you will be the Reiki Alchemist who by using all these tools will effect a change on some level for your Client, whom or whatever that may be. Undoubtedly a change for the better! Reiki can never cause harm.

The true and unlimited nature of energy is not yet fully understood. Every *thing* that is in existence in our Universe, is on the basic level vibrating creating energy. Can you see it, touch it or taste it? I invite you to explain or imagine its limits. You will find you probably are unable to, but energy can however be harnessed and used through modalities or tools such as Reiki and the other methods or items that will be described and taught in this book. This book cannot begin to define Energy-we only skim the surface of its applications based on the modalities we will be learning and using. Hence a lay person unfamiliar with Alchemical concepts would not realize that energy can equal a change that some may regard as magical or outside the realms of possibility. Energy modalities can alter the way you perceive this Reality. Energy is how you as the student will effect change by its application with your intention (Spiritual), laying on of hands (Physical) or by using your limitless powerful mind (Transcendence) to imagine the CHANGE (Alchemy) which in turn becomes your Alchemical formula. Reading, learning and using these ideas related to using the Reiki and other modalities (Energy) will also effect a change in *YOU* on all those levels. How? By working with it, growing in the knowledge and using it on a daily basis. Energy work becomes intriguing and you will begin to master the use of it the longer you work with it and learn it. Your mind will learn how others perceive it and use it and you may think of many new ways to apply your personal knowledge and gifts. Remember our minds are an unlimited energy source also and our most powerful gift! New synapses will form allowing the Reiki to flow throughout. Your mind will be expanded in new ways that will astound and amaze you. ***Remember I said this.*** In the next year as you look back at where you were at that point in time and then realize how you have grown into an amazing **Alchemical Light Worker.** Your gifts will bring new growth and insights on a continuous basis. Transcending old thoughts, actions and overcoming any inherent fear will determine how you progress in this knowledge. Everyone has their own perceptions based on their past, their experiences and their willingness and interest to learn new things and apply that new formula to your life.

Universal Life Energy would be our American translation of the word Reiki. The actual meaning of the word Reiki in Japanese is healing, and the word Reiki was in common usage which is why Dr. Usui named his method the Usui Shiki Ryoho Reiki method to separate it and name it as his own. This method or modality was first known to have been used in Japan by Dr. Usui (who was at that time among other life paths -a Buddhist monk.) He was compelled to retreat for some time on a mountaintop meditating and receiving the symbols that are used to "command" or "call the energies. He received the enhancements- as the symbols were to the energy of Reiki -when they appeared to him and he began to use them and teach them along with the hand placements in his method. I visualize an enlightened, fasting, tired man meditating and the symbols and usage intuitively appearing to him in his mind's eye. Do I know this for a fact? No, and this book is not about the history of the esteemed Dr. There are many books and/or online sites dedicated for further researches if you are interested in the basic foundations of Reiki and its first Teacher. Let me add this also with regard to the history or foundation of the Usui system: Hawayo Takata another famous Reiki Master, after coming to death's door and being healed by Dr. Usui's Reiki method in Japan brought Reiki to the Western world via coming back to her home in Hawaii and it has grown or evolved from her teachings also. She brought the symbols and began to teach this energy work to others. The lineage of Reiki or the foundations of Reiki came from these, other Reiki Masters and students of these Reiki pioneers. The Gakkai (a lay Buddhist association affiliated with teachings of Nichiren) of Japan still carry on a faithful and as far as can be determined un-distilled version of Dr. Usui's Reiki. Today there are many schools or teachings all over the world. In the beginning as I understand it, Dr. Usui attuned persons attending his groups (at this point I don't believe he was teaching his method yet outside the Gakkai). Many people came because this Reiju (in Japanese this implies a conferment and a receipt of the energy) as the attunement is known was given. There were over 60 chapters but after WWII the membership dropped drastically. This was just a brief synopsis so that you are familiar with who we in America base our teachings from. Lineage is important because there are no acknowledged (by the Government and medical communities) accredited schools for Reiki at this time. Reiki Master Teachers pass this knowledge on so that you may be perceived as Certified and recognized by authority. Clients may ask how you got where you are. You will also receive Certification from whomever becomes your Reiki Master Teacher. There are four levels. I will also talk about Lineage as it relates to the Chakra system. Dr. Usui definitively indicated that this was the method to develop the lineage for the practitioner. One of the reasons I am mentioning this because as with anything that is perceived as a business and takes monies from Clients, should you choose that Path, be careful not to be deceitful in any way as far as acknowledgement of where you learned Reiki and any information you share with your Clients in that regard.

Where did the Reiki come from originally? Reiki is a gift of energy coming from the Source or higher power whatever you may call that higher power perhaps even the recently discovered "God particle'? This particular modality utilizing three Japanese script-based symbols was given to Dr. Usui through inspiration and has since been shared worldwide. Buddhism has been in existence long before Christianity. I am saying this because I got into a conversation with a devout Christian speaking about Reiki and she was afraid of it as not being from God or even Reiki being of a "spiritual" nature. Had Dr. Usui been a Christian perhaps the symbols would have been based on Christian words or script whatever they may be. I would caution people in general to know that Reiki is energy and has no "faith" per se although it is considered a gift of the spirit. The Bible itself was not written in this woman's language originally either however she believes in it. So, perhaps those examples should be kept in mind and the realization that Reiki is not demonized if that is what she was indeed thinking. You can NEVER hurt anyone with Reiki. Any person that I have ever met who used Reiki did so with a loving intention. Now I am sharing how I express it and apply it, with you. There are those also who scoff at the entire idea of holistic modalities in their entirety and they too have a right to their opinion although I will say there are more things "unseen" than we can ever hope to know as history has shown. There are so many examples to choose from. Scientifically, how about germs? Not long ago, their existence was not even known, and people thought evil spirits could cause sickness among other- strange to us beliefs, so when you as a new Practitioner get asked these questions perhaps you could keep these simple examples in mind as an answer. These modalities that I will share with you are not considered religious in nature. They are just that – a modality or tool we will learn to utilize to help ourselves and others. Many do consider the modality of Reiki sacred considering the Source however, if you are not of a spiritual nature the modality will still work because it is pure energy. You- nor your Client(s) have to believe in it for it to work. Reiki transcends all peoples, places, things, religions, governments, possibilities. Pure energy is the essence of Reiki. It works through thought or through physicality and/or both simultaneously. When you have been working with these energies for as long as I have you will realize how astounding it is to be able to "harness" these energies and tools. Reiki is a priceless gift to each of us.

Reiki in Japan is not thought of in the same way as it is in the United States. Here mostly we synonymously think of it as this Usui system of healing. In Japan there are many systems that are identified with the word *reiki* and Japanese people also have a mindset or philosophy tied in with this, similar to a philosophy that I base my life and the way I think on which is called HUNA from the Hawaiian word meaning secret because it was kept secret from all who weren't of Hawaiian lineage for many centuries. There is another word: *ho'omana* and it is the true name of the philosophy and way of life of the Hawaiian peoples. Briefly to understand HUNA you would need to know that it is based on seven precepts which are:

1. IKE – The world is what you think it is.

2. KALA – There are no limits.

3. MAIKA – Energy flows where attention goes.

4. MANAWA – Now is the moment of power.

5. ALOHA – To love is to be happy with.

6. MANA – All power comes from within.

7. PONO – Effectives is the measure of truth.

Meditation on them will help you understand the basics. To really know HUNA you would need to make a life study of it. These seven precepts along with the understanding of the inner self or body-mind (Unihipili), the ego (Uhane), and the higher self (Aumakua) allows you to become unified and able to experience Aloha and how this philosophy works. HUNA is the perfect example of Alchemy using your mind and intention. HUNA also has a healing component that you can work into your practice and daily life. Breathing is essential so in HUNA you create MANA (energy) by breathing. You take in a breath deeply hold it and blow it out with a HA! sound. You do this four times once to honor Uni, once to honor Uhane, once to honor Aumakua and once to honor either the Source or the Universe. You can do this set of four once prior to doing a treatment. If you need a lot of energy you can do sets of four however many times you may be guided to. This breathing can also help as a source of energy to you throughout your day. Mostly we are all shallow breathers, so it makes sense the more oxygen you have the more energy you will be able to tap. Breathing is a key component in Yoga for example.

In Japan how Reiki is known is roughly translated as the three diamonds which are: Earth, heart and head, each part thereof a diamond then forming a triangle if you can picture that in your mind. To put this in its simplest terms you do this by grounding yourself through a series of meditations and bringing into alignment your heart and head and higher self. HUNA speaks of this also as in aligning your inner self or subconscious (Uni), your conscious self (Uhane) and your superconscious (Aumakua). We are not going into depth at this point but will interweave these thoughts throughout the classes. In any case it is always a good thing to have ourselves grounded and all our "selves" in alignment.

You may also ask "What is grounding or what do you mean by that term"? Good question. Grounding is a spiritual term for a feeling of being physically "connected" to earth-a sense of being here on this plane. By going outside in nature, we will help ourselves to "ground" as will the act of visualizing ourselves here and now on the earth. I also like to do a meditation visualizing what I call the Tree of Life® which goes something like this: Go outside (weather permitting) bare feet if possible, breathe deeply and slowly, close your eyes, place your feet about shoulder width apart, slightly bent at the knee and raising your arms to wherever is comfortable for you for a few minutes. Raise your face to the heavens and visualize the roots of the great Tree going down, down deep into the earth through dirt and rock growing towards the center, then picture the nourishment or energy of the earth coming up through the roots through the thickness of the trunk, up the Tree and out into the branches and leaves. Allow the sun's energy also to permeate the leaves and feel that energy flowing down to meet the energies of the earth thereby co-mingling and the Tree becomes a conduit of energy – YOU ARE THE TREE- just stand there feeling these energies until you are feeling deeply, spiritually connected to everything physical. Breathe deeply and open your eyes when you are ready. My students usually love this meditation and many of them have told me later they use it on a continuous basis. Of course, when we do it in person it is slower, and I am guiding it however you can do it for yourself too. Also, another way you can "ground" is by visualizing a thick, great chain being tied to the center of the earth going outward and attaching to your physical body. When we work with Spirit we can lose that attachment and feel or act flighty or unconnected to the physical plane. Eating can also help us feel grounded so after a treatment it is a good idea to have a healthy snack and drink plenty of water for the Practitioner and the Client. Grounding and/or using those energies enable us to clear our Chakra system. We will learn briefly about Chakras, what they do and how to work with them later on. Our Mother earth, Gaia, also has Chakras.

REIKI

My thought is that any person who "lays" hands on another is using a form of this Reiki energy whatever name they choose to call it. Perhaps they know nothing of the Reiki symbols however they are using the energy. In my own mind I think many holy men perhaps even including Jesus and his disciples could have been using this energy for their healing work. I believe Healing Touch is similar however, they do not utilize the symbols but they do use the energy. It all comes down to intention. What is the true intention of the person trying to effect a change with Energy? Reiki is not a religion- it is a non-discriminatory tool to be used to help others and you, situations, animals etc. We are, as all things are, composed of energy as proved in quantum physics and an accepted fact in scientific circles. Moreover, it stands to reason that energy applied to energy effects some type of change – some might call it a healing at the least it may be a change for the better or there may be other names for it. Basically, the work yields some type of Alchemical formula which in turn causes an Alchemical reaction allowing you to effect a change. It is up to each individual to decide that for themselves. I know that I can feel the energy and have seen changes effected on many levels. It certainly feels wonderful. Underlying stress is the reason that dis-ease manifests so if we can get our bodies and minds to a state of relaxation our bodies' instinctual natural healing abilities begin to function. Any type of "medicine" is in effect helping your body to heal itself. Western medicine provides drugs, surgery, rehabilitation as some examples, however any modality be it Western or holistic all basically do the same thing- effect some sort of change so the body can do the work to get back to its own perfection.

I decided to write this book as a compendium of the tools I use for myself when teaching my classes and for others who were looking for something out of the ordinary that goes in a somewhat different direction *transcending* what they may have read about Reiki & other energy work up to this point. Of course, I have not read every book and they all have value however this one is tailored for my specifications. I consider myself Shamanistic in thought and needed something that would encompass the way I teach, think and do my work. My sincere desire is that this book will help you in your work and perhaps show you some new ways in which to focus the direction that your work might take or how you may choose to teach your own classes. I will say Reiki is the central energetic tool we are using and the other modalities are choices that can be added to the Reiki treatment some or all of the time depending on what you are comfortable with and that you resonate with. What do I mean? I find a lot of people are not comfortable with or are not attracted to all the things that I do or use especially dowsing with the pendulum. That is perfectly fine although I will say as a diagnostic tool the pendulum is irreplaceable to me. You may incorporate other methods into your work. The methods that I am teaching about here are the ones that I am using up to this point in time and will continue to use even if I add others. Let me add this: sometimes those things which we struggle with are our greatest lessons so please do keep that in mind when trying these new modalities. Some of them may go against ingrained religious inhibitions or seem as if they should not be considered as part of what you would like to learn. Please do keep an open mind. The Universe offers us many paths and it is always up to us which of those we will tread. By opening the door to the idea of adding these modalities or tools; the seed is planted and perhaps you as the practitioner will become more open to using new approaches while remaining fluid which is absolutely *vital* when working with humanity. Your own Alchemical formula will be based on your knowledge, perceptions and the tools you choose to use.

One of the basic questions I love to ask people who come for class or a treatment is "What is the first thing you do when you get hurt or have a headache?" Most of the time I get an answer similar to "I touch that area.' Why? By placing your hands there you are generating energy and it feels good. Hugs feel wonderful! Along with the basics of life Humans and other life need touch to sustain it on every level. Touch is a physical, spiritual and mental requirement for this plane of existence. It has become another scientific fact that Humans and animals require touch to thrive at any age! We have initially come to the earth to experience the physical reality and of course, to work on whatever "lessons" that we have chosen beforehand.

Basically, Reiki is activating energy by touching (unless of course the client specifically does not want or cannot be touched and that is ok too because even if we do not touch them physically the energy is touching them and activated on some level because of intention and symbols). Otherwise you can place your hands in the air above their body or by means of a symbol from Level II you can send Reiki and still get the same effect as if you were touching or using the energy. Most people are comfortable with the treatment once the process is explained and perhaps even demonstrated at first so there are no surprises. Let me clarify the word client here also. Client means any person, animal, place, situation or thing that you are using the Reiki energy on or for. Reiki energy and the subject or situation that you may use it on is only limited by your imagination! There truly are no limits when it comes to this energy. If you think of it you can do it. The entire Universe is comprised of energy! So to me that means you can use Reiki on everything. Yes, I did say everything! Amazing isn't it? Also, since in the precepts of HUNA "There are no limits" and you will hear this over and over in my classes – the usage of Reiki is only limited by YOUR imagination! Putting it in its' simplest terms Reiki is energy. What you are learning is how to apply it and how to become the channel or pipeline for the energy either through your hands or your mind. Therefore it is another good resource to go to Reiki shares and get new ideas or go online and read some of the Reiki pages and there are groups there you can share with also. Many minds bring new and exciting ways to use the energy.

Have the Reiki teachings stayed true to the basic foundations? My answer would have to be yes, and even though I myself learned in two different schools of thought- the basic foundation remained. The first Reiki Master Teacher (RMT) that I had taught the sacred way going back to the original Usui school of thought and lineage meaning that the symbols could not be written down or shown to anyone who was not in process of learning or had the attunements (these will be discussed later). The symbols had to be drawn precisely with no variations. We drew them in sand and if we drew them on paper they had to be burned and flushed. Imagine that these days!

Considering those methods, I now know this personally was good training for the memory and committing a precise thought or idea to mind. In our world today where it seems as if there is very little reverence for anything, this gave me an insight into that way of honoring something. A lot of the Reiki that I do is in the mind. Shamanistic thought does not allow the limitation of time/space which is a human construct, therefore it also fits right in with the fact that I can use a symbol from the second level and send Reiki to past/present/future and my ability to work with energy in any dimension also is unlimited. ***Allow yourself to consider those possibilities for a moment***. The fact is simply ***astounding*** that you can spend a lifetime at this and still not cover all the possibilities. All the Reiki Masters on the entire planet could not begin to cover the unlimited resources this enables us to work with! A truly simple example of this would be an upcoming job interview you or another may have scheduled at a future date. You would invoke the distance symbol from level II and send Reiki to that specific time, date, persons involved, place involved etc. also using the rest of your symbols asking for the highest good for all concerned. The possibilities are unlimited. You are only limited by your own imagination as I have stated before. Will you get that job? I cannot promise that as the job may not be in your best interest however, you will do your best and who knows you may get an even better position with the same company or you can be assured the possibilities are endless and whatever is right for that situation will manifest. Now, using another example we cannot change the past per se, however we can have the intention to change the emotion of the past. We can send Reiki to the past memory asking to release the painful emotion, take the lesson and move forward from there. This is particularly effective for unhappiness or perhaps abuse cases. In those scenarios we are affecting some type of movement or change however that may happen. Can we predict the outcome? No. We are sending energy to a situation and hoping for a specific outcome but there are many variables that need to be taken into account, so the outcome depends on all those things. We must also have learned that Reiki goes where it will. No one has a certainty as to where or what it will affect. I believe but am not certain that since Reiki originated from the Source then perhaps it has some ingrained consciousness that directs it to the deepest levels of energy where it is needed. That is only a personal opinion and unproven scientifically although there are some studies in progress at this time. In many cases, I have seen the desired outcome but sometimes not. My thoughts on this comes under the heading of the "Big Picture" as we cannot always know what is best in terms of the highest good similar to an unanswered prayer not really being unanswered. It just means that the answer was this particular pathway is not open to you at this time. It may not be in our best interest and we cannot see it for ourselves. How often does that happen?

In Reiki, going back to the Usui method, we would learn a specific placement for our hands which covers the Endocrine system. The modern way is to use those placements as a basis and tuning in to the person by diagnosing, scanning and intention we will place our hands in other areas as we are guided to do so. Reiki should flow. The entire idea is to get the energy flowing through the Chakras and through the crown down to the feet and vice versa.

The initial hand positions I learned were a dozen in number covering the endocrine system as compared to a more fluid intuitive approach today and flowed from one to the other and were precisely placed. We went over and over them. Those Level I and II classes gave me a great foundation and allowed me to build solidly on what I had learned. I came out of those classes able to do the hand placements and the symbols without referring to anything written. That Teacher was one of my greatest Mentors and I highly recommend you find someone to nurture you in gaining knowledge also. Throughout your Spiritual/Work life you should always look for or have a Mentor. This has become my understanding and advice. We can always benefit from someone wiser than ourselves and with different knowledge. There are many wise people out there giving classes, writing books and who are willing to share what they know. When you are ready you will be attracted to that particular path but remembering to always use discernment when spending your hard-earned money that the person you are trusting is worthy also. Everyone has an agenda~ even you and me! Just make sure it is in line with yours. Recently I read about a psychic who stole millions from her clients abusing the gift she was given and hurting all those others who are true and are here to help us. The truth will out in every case eventually. To avoid this hurt, you need to be discerning and ask for help from your Guides, Angels & Enlightened Beings. Don't be afraid to question anything especially when your hard-earned money is involved. Also remembering that none of us is perfect and hopefully whomever it is you are dealing with will strive to fulfill what you expect from them as long as your expectations are within reason.

I then took Advanced (Level III) and my Master Level class from another RMT who was more modern in her thinking and one of her explanations of this was that a person seeing the symbols written down would not know what to do with them anyway although I still consider them sacred and try to hold them so. I learned much more flexibility, how to use my intuition and how to be more open in incorporating other "tools" into my treatments from her. She was very gifted and taught me a lot about intuition and being uninhibited in using my gifts. People are not always comfortable when you speak of working with Angels, Guides and Fairies (these are other energies that are available to us)! I am truly grateful that I had both of these wonderful women available to me at the right time when I was ready. Spirit and Universal connectedness guides us when we develop our intuition which is another powerful tool in energy work. Sometimes especially when we ask and are ready Spirit will lead us to our next Teacher.

One thing I do not agree with and perhaps I am old fashioned is that I do not think you can teach yourself and give yourself the Attunements as I have seen being offered online. You need to take a class and have a Certified RMT teach you Reiki. You of course can research and learn as much as you are able before you take a class, however you need to physically take the classes. There are certain requirements that need to be met to become an RMT although these are much more lax than they used to be. You really need to see how others do the Reiki and get the Attunement in person. The Attunement is a "gift" from RMT to the student. The symbols are placed into the student's aura. Therefore, a student cannot do this for themselves regardless of what is advertised online or via a book. One reason for the Attunement is developing lineage. In the past, lineage was very important as it described your roots and who you were. We don't seem to focus on that these days, but I am adamant that you must learn Reiki in person. By getting an Attunement in person that in turn, allows the Reiki to flow through the lineage also. I am still learning each time I go to a Reiki share and also when I read different articles and talk to other RMT's about how they practice. You will be happy you took the classes in person if for nothing else than the hands-on practice. Also, if you do not network or see Reiki in person how will you know you are doing it correctly even though it has become more fluid? An added bonus is you get to meet people of like mind. It is my certain knowledge that the Attunements should be given in person by a Certified RMT who in turn has been given theirs the same way. This is how Lineage is developed. I liken it to the Chakra system and how the energy flows through it. Dr. Usui gave us Reiki becoming the Root Chakra and each person who was attuned after becomes part of that Reiki Chakra energy system or the lineage of Reiki. These are only my interpretations of that subject. Dr. Usui himself indicated that this was the way Reiki had to be passed on from teacher to student. So I honor this. Your RMT becomes your Mentor and should become a co-worker on the path of Light.

Our usage and understanding of Reiki has evolved in some ways. No-*thing* stays the same. Everything is in flux all the time. Life flows forward and so must we. In order to survive in modern times and to encompass the myriad possibilities we must grow and morph so too must our usage of our knowledge of Reiki. The basic foundations are there to be built on and the symbols are what they are. They have been in use for many years. They have a consciousness of their own and they know their name whether it is by the intention of the person using them or some other fashion they come when called no exceptions. They do their intended work no exceptions. Do we always know what that work is? NO. We cannot direct it. We are only the channel that allows the Reiki energy to flow and it goes where it will. That is why when I am doing Reiki I use ALL my symbols ALL the time. Why? This is part my formula for success. I want my Client to achieve the highest possible outcome so my Alchemical formula includes as many tools as possible.

It is not up to me to discern what exactly is needed or what I may think is needed. How would I know? I can only see the surface and while I may claim to be intuitive I am not All-knowing or All-powerful (darn!). So I cover all my bases and

I use all of them as I said. I know that some RMT's use certain ones at certain times. I do not agree with this especially dealing with another human being although I will say that if you do all your symbols and then you wish to use a particular one in a certain area of the body then do it. We cannot see their past/present/future so we obviously came to this work because we wanted to help people, so this is my simple solution. Never assume you know what is best always use the best of your knowledge and ability without judgment. Truly become the channel. Take your EGO out of the picture.

Also, do not become a fanatic about it. Be balanced as you should be in all things. Yes, this work is exciting and a blessing however, I have seen people who get carried away in their pursuit of this path and by their very intensity turn people off. Discernment is key as I seem to keep harping on. Consider the situation without EGO and taking all things into account decide if it is fortuitous to mention or offer Reiki. You do not have to get accolades and get patted on the back all the time in public. You can do Reiki very effectively quietly and with no one the wiser as long as you have asked for permission in your mind. I have a list that I do every morning for remote healing. Sometimes people will pop into my mind or I know others have asked me to do this and I include them on this list to receive Reiki remotely. Remote healing involves using a symbol from Level II to "send" the energy to whomever or whatever you wish to work on. You can also ask for the energy to be sent on a continuous flow throughout a specified period of time or to that person's Angels who will then send the Reiki as needed to their charge. I also "charge" the water of my shower with Reiki symbols with the intention that the Reiki will flow continuously until the next shower. I am a water baby (Cancer) so when I work with or in water it seems to enhance whatever it is that I am doing. I then send this energy to the earth, all beings on or around it, myself, a list of people for remote healing and to the Angels and other spirit beings for themselves and to use for their Charges. As I remind you, there are no limits.

Another hard and fast rule to become a Reiki provider - You as the provider of the service can make suggestions of a non-medical nature, however NEVER are you to diagnose, offer medical advice or suggest to anyone they do not need any type of Western medicine. Holistic modalities are never to replace modern medicine <u>at your suggestion</u>. You will never be qualified to make that judgment no matter how many classes you take, how many books you read, how intuitive you are unless you become a Doctor and I cannot emphasize this strongly enough. This is a human being's life we are talking about. The services you are offering are an enhancement never a replacement. These people are coming to you in trust- be worthy of it. Being a Reiki provider is not about owning power~ it is about serving. You will also open yourself up to legal issues if you do so. (Another note here if you plan to open a practice it is a good idea to have some type of insurance coverage). If a formal treatment is given it is good to have a "disclaimer statement" (see an example on page 93) signed by the client to cover yourself. It is also important to maintain discretion, morality and ethics in your practice no matter where or when it is. There is never to be any sexuality involved in this. I usually make it a practice to cover my client with a sheet or blanket thereby "de-sexing" them and making them more comfortable. This is especially important to those clients who have abuse issues. We always have to try to be cognizant of all these things while trying to maintain empathy and a sincere desire to be of service. It is a fine line to walk. There are laws on the books specific to the difference between Reiki and for instance, Massage in NY State where I happen to reside. So, it is up to you and/or your teacher to make you aware of these things. Above all our goal is to maintain the sacred good "name" of Reiki and the good name of those wonderful people who have invested all that is required to help others, learn this modality and become Certified in it. Also, we can never claim to HEAL out in the world at large. Reiki is for stress relief only which in turn allows the body to heal itself. The human body is a wonderful machine and it can heal itself under the right conditions. When there is no stress, the body can return to its own perfection however that might look in this reality. Unfortunately, your Reiki certification does not come with a red cape or a wand! You are not the healer – the body is. Do not overstep your bounds. You will only hurt yourself and the others you started out trying to help in the first place not to mention opening yourself up to lawsuits if you claim to "Heal". Integrity is absolutely vital to becoming a practitioner.

All these modalities require a complete retraining of your mind. We all have been taught from early childhood that a lot of these things that cannot be seen or measured are not real. We are essentially developing our unused 6th sense or opening our 3rd eye. This energy work is an on-going process. Believe me when I tell you that I have been doing this work for fifteen years seriously and most of my life generally and I still get caught up in old ways of thinking. I am constantly questioning myself. Perhaps it is this that keeps each one of us on that "right" path. Nurture your particular gifts and they will grow. The path becomes like the analogy of the tree in that you plant the tree and the roots grow first thus laying the foundation and pretty soon the seedling sprouts and slowly the trunk begins to form, eventually branching out and growing leaves and perhaps even flowers or nuts like me! Know that it will not happen overnight. Once you open the door the light of understanding will begin to shine and as you are meant to your path will become clearer to you. You may not be destined to become a healer (knowing that when I use this term I do not mean that you are a Dr. or to claim you can heal someone, my meaning is similar to that of an ASSISTANT and CHANNEL). You may just be interested in the work in a general way just for yourself or your family and/or your pets. That is fine. However you feel called is the right way. I am asking you also never compare yourself to others. The Universe is a diverse place and so too should we honor diversity. We all have unique gifts and are all called to express them in different ways. We are all where we are supposed to be NOW! I am smiling when I say this so too should you be.

Knowledge is never wasted and whatever you do is perfect for you at this time. Many times I have learned something, purchased a book or taken a class and have not used the information at that particular time only to find myself coming back to it when it was more appropriate and I really needed it. I find books on my shelves all the time that I do not remember buying but there they are and are relevant at that time.

In order to become a more effective Light Worker as I call myself (and this is a phrase I picked up from George Noory, a favorite author), I have added many "tools" to what he called "my tool box" when working with people. I have my formula all worked out, however if I learn something new I add it so the formula is constantly being tweaked. So, harking back to evolution, I would have to say that I am not purely an RMT anymore perhaps as Dr. Usui or Mrs. Takata understood it my work *transcends* traditional Reiki with the usage of additional modalities and fulfills the idea of an Alchemical formula. I view myself as an Alchemist Shaman stepping outside time/space and incorporating any ideas, modalities and I use whatever works. I am intuitive and I do have some standard practices that I use EVERY time I do a treatment.

THE REIKI TREATMENT

Initially when a person has come to me for help I will sit down with them and I may take notes (which will remain confidential) and please note carefully- never will I discuss this person's name or any of their personal information. I may share general information in a class as to how I chose to do that particular treatment or I may ask my client if I may share generalities ahead of time. This comes under that directive of asking permission meaning it is not up to us to interfere on another person's path even if they are suffering unless we have permission. It is a good idea to find out why the person thinks they have come to you to begin with. Many times I find that the reason they have come is NOT the reason they are really there. There may be a symptom or a host of symptoms; however there is usually a larger underlying issue that may need to be addressed or not depending on how the session or sessions happen. The client may feel better after a session or series of sessions but if the underlying issues remain (i.e. the way of thinking) they probably will go right back to the dis-ease. This can become quite disheartening to all concerned. You can only do your best. Just know that Reiki works on levels that we do not yet fully understand. I have had clients like this and have seen changes happen much later and I felt that the changes were initiated by Reiki. So, we can never know at what point Reiki will work. Since linear time is a construct of human thought and does not really exist except in our minds so then it follows that Reiki is working at any given time. We just need to trust that we are doing the work we are meant to do and the client is getting the energy they are meant to and whatever happens after that is out of our hands. Reiki does have its own consciousness and we or at least I do not entirely understand all the dimensions of the energy and when you throw Angels and Guides into the mix well things can become pretty interesting. You need to realize too that while you have a "team" your client does also. Also, we as Souls are here on a certain path so too we must keep that in the back of our minds. You can only do your best, stay as detached but compassionate as possible whilst still being an Alchemical Light Worker and remember to also give yourself Reiki – you deserve it!

Every single Reiki session that I have ever participated in has been different even with the same person! This is still amazing to me. The basic treatment stays the same although the approach may change. As you grow on your path you will begin to discern and learn what formula may be needed and you will become a student of humanity and our foibles.

Let me also say here that I mentally & physically prepare myself for doing Reiki by doing HUNA (Hawaiian philosophy) breathing and I also try to "tune-in" to that person. I do this by closing my eyes and using my inner self which is connected to all things on some level. I will ask to be connected to that person, place, animal or thing. A prayer or brief meditation can work also. I also ground myself using the previously mentioned meditation based on the Tree analogy that I teach to my students during class. I do not claim to be psychic although I do sometimes get insights or see things~ it is not consistent. I will say I am intuitive instead. I do connect with the person. My Angels and Guides also come to work with me and the person who has come to me for help also has Angels and Guides. Sometimes I am gifted to channel information. I also prepare the area where I am doing Reiki with whatever it is I will be using such as music, crystals, essential oils, etc and of course, I cleanse it physically and spiritually using the Reiki symbols. I also wash my hands before and after. I use clean sheets on my table and have a box of tissues ready and water for drinking. Now, some people will not have a dedicated place for Reiki and that is ok too. You as the practitioner can use your Power symbol (you will learn all the symbols in Reiki II) and cleanse the area in your mind or physically prior to the treatment if on the "fly" so to speak. Then proceed to do the best you can wherever you are. I have heard this called "band-aid" Reiki as you may not be able to do a full treatment but may just be doing a treatment at a specific area of the body for example if someone had a broken bone. You can do an effective treatment while someone is sitting in a chair or lying on their own bed. Remaining fluid is the key to becoming an effective Reiki practitioner.

The body manifests dis-ease for many reasons and most of the time it does not happen overnight. Dis-ease is a direct result of our thought processes. Yes, I had a very difficult time with this concept also. Some of these thought processes may be inherited from your environmental upbringing or your genetic imprinting. I myself had to manifest dis-ease to get this concept. Let me tell you that I got SO indignant, angry and depressed when I got diagnosed with several forms of arthritis because after all I AM a Reiki Master Teacher, Spiritual leader of a sort (or so I think) and have studied many modalities for years and how could this be so? After much meditation, soul searching and praying I have come to the conclusion that this has happened so I would get this concept and also be open to be more forgiving of myself and my humanity which in turn allows me to do the same for others. Also, I find that our experience seems to draw those to us with similar experience because we can empathize with those whom we can understand. Change your mind change your life has always been one of my guiding manifestos so this is always something I work on and who knows someday I may get to the root and be completely healed of dis-ease. One other thing I would like to say here DO NOT own the dis-ease. Never say "MY" or "I AM" with regards to dis-ease whatever it is. That places it in the subconscious mind as yours and the subconscious mind is very literal. Always say "the" whatever it may be. This is a retraining of thinking also. I catch myself all the time in this manner and once you begin to become aware of it you will also. Do not become the dis-ease and do not identify with it. This is quite difficult to do especially when you live with a chronic condition. Do the best you can. Just remember to love yourself and all the rest will fall into place. Every day is a new day and we must try to live in the NOW as it is the only real time we have. Also note that "I AM" are creation words so anything you state after those words comes into being. Be very careful to only state positives after those words and you will manifest amazing results! My favorite affirmation from Louise L. Hay is: "I AM an unlimited being accepting in unlimited ways from unlimited resources and I AM grateful". Doesn't that cover it all?

THE ENERGY BODY

A basic understanding of the energy body is a good place to start learning how to begin an intuitive diagnosis to help you know where you may want to concentrate some extra attention during treatment time. We all have what is called the AURA. This is our energy or etheric body. The AURA surrounds our body and is a sort of a shadow body perhaps extending out anywhere from a few inches to a foot or so in all directions around the outside of the body although some people have extremely large AURAS and you can tell them by their gift of Charisma. We can train ourselves to project or pull-in our AURA if we so desire. This can be useful in certain situations. Some people are gifted to "see" the AURA and manifestations of dis-ease before we may be aware of them.

Some examples of projection being useful might be if you were giving a speech or teaching a class you would want your audience to connect with you, so you could consciously project your AURA to make the connection with theirs. On the other hand, perhaps you may be in a situation where you may not want to be noticed so you could detract your AURA and pull it in tightly to your body thus disengaging from any surrounding beings. When you consider these examples you may have already done so without knowing what it was that you were doing. As I said before, some of us are gifted in the fact that we are able to "see" our own and other AURAS. I can see it however I do not often see the colors much to my everlasting chagrin and ongoing effort. I do know some who are gifted in that respect. They can see a lot of the colors and changes which indicate dis-ease or other issues in the energy body. The AURA can become a complete study in itself as there are a rainbow of colors and meanings which I am not going into at this time. I do have a couple of exercises that I can use in my class to help my students get a sense of the AURA, what it is, how it feels and how to work with it. Once we have done these exercises and my students have "seen" or at least "felt" the AURA or not (occasionally this happens). Sometimes it takes quite a few attempts and training to do this. Using my hands I scan the AURA as part of my diagnostic process prior to doing a treatment. This can be called AURIC scanning. You place your hands about 6-12 inches above the persons' body with your hands extended outward from your body comfortably and hands about 4 inches apart start at the head and scan down each side slowly, closing your eyes and really trying to feel and tune into that person. You may feel sensations of temperature, pain, visuals or some other indications of what may be going on in that persons' body. The energetic body is a reflection of the physical body. Since you do not have X-ray vision this is the next best thing!

Auric scanning is really a tool that you develop intuitively, and you are putting your hands right into someone's AURA or energy body sometimes called the Etheric body. If you quiet your mind, close your eyes and "tune-in" directing your thoughts and senses towards the person you are working on you will feel sensations. How you interpret them will depend on how far you are on your path. If you are new then pay particular attention, remember what happened and where; and then ask the client discreetly without alarming them perhaps something like this for example: "Client A I noticed some heat in the lower part of your back and when you came you mentioned that you had been experiencing some pain, so I am going to do some extra Reiki there. I also recommend you follow up with your family Physician or a Chiropractor. I also get the sense that you are feeling overwhelmed by some burden that is weighing you down. I am going to do a short meditation with you and ask that this burden be lifted from you to relieve your back." Remember I told you that dis-ease usually begins in our minds. Perhaps Client A will get relief from this meditation, the Reiki and/or going to the Dr. or Chiropractor or some combination thereof. You can only offer the best of your thoughts and abilities. This is an example of an Alchemical formula. Please do not be intimidated. If you are reading this you probably have some life experience. Apply it and common sense in your Reiki practice. Use your discernment and people skills also. However, DO NOT ASSUME. That was just an example. Auric scanning is a tool that can be developed over time using it over and over. It is a powerful diagnostic tool to connect at a deep level with your client because you do have your AURA mixing with their AURA. Universally we are all connected on some level anyway however this connection really allows you to tap into knowledge that is vital to helping your Client. At the time of treatment, we can also ask the "Team" to guide us in knowledge for the Client. Now this may seem strange to you however I "talk" to my Angels & Guides directly telepathically to exchange information and get intuitive guidance. Many people get "feelings" or intuitions that can help guide them however we must remember to take EGO out of it and sometimes just let things flow. Sometimes you may get feelings in your hands when placed on an area, you may get a visualization, or you may get some intuitive knowledge. All these things can grow as you grow in your work. To reiterate, Reiki goes where it will so my thoughts on this idea are that Reiki goes to the macrocosmic level and begins working there whilst it may also work on something specific that you have directed it to.

CHAKRAS

We begin working on understanding more of the energy body called the CHAKRAS. The word Chakra comes from Sanskrit (India) meaning Wheel. Chakras are invisible unless you are gifted with being able to "see" them which is quite uncommon as far as I know. I am able to "see" them using dowsing and get information regarding the flow of energy. The Chakras are the basis of my diagnostic process along with Auric scanning. It is important to get as much information as possible. Each one has its own color, its own spin and they each relate to certain areas, dis-ease or issues of the body as well as having other applications. There are 7 major Chakras that most people work with and smaller ones in each hand and foot however there are also 5 other Chakras over and above these. I mention them just so you are aware of them and perhaps may learn more about them at a later date if you continue on to become a Reiki Master Teacher. The Chakra systems connects us to the Universe and allows the energy to flow from the earth up through us out the Crown to the Universe thus effectively connecting us to Everything and vice versa. In my classes I have my students color a chart showing the 7 chakras we work with so they can get a sense of each one and coloring gives the subconscious mind that impression for each one. I also have a large Chart that shows each system and we talk about what each Chakra does and what systems it corresponds to. A simple quick guide is to think of a Rainbow with the red coming up from the earth going through each color until you reach the violet at the crown of the head with the rest of the colors in between. There are many great books if you wish further studies into Chakras. It seems as if once you begin studying Reiki and start learning about energy you may become overwhelmed at the wealth of information. You have a lifetime to learn. Take your time and learn what you are interested in. Just knowing the Chakra system exists and what each one represents is a great start. It is here in the Chakra system that you can do some of your most effective work. The energy needs to be flowing in order for the Client to be healthy. You may begin this work with the Tree Meditation ® for yourself and/or others.

Each Chakra has a corresponding color. Colors are a property of light which in turn is a Vibration and energy. Colors can affect our health, inner harmony and emotions. Color is a living energy. Remember I said every *thing* vibrates and is energy.

- ***RED stimulates the brain wave activity, increases heart rate, respirations and blood pressure, excites sexual glands. RED energizes the 1st Chakra (root or coccyx). RED warms us and awakes us physically and energizes our blood. RED is good to wear for colds and poor circulation. Too much***

RED can overstimulate as it is the color of passion. High blood pressure is one example of too much RED energy in your body. RED is the color of war, prosperity, fire and the rising sun. Spiritually it is the root color of fire and connects us to our physical self. Red as the root chakra means : I AM.

- *ORANGE is a color of joy and wisdom. ORANGE affects the 2nd Chakra (sacral). ORANGE gives energy, stimulates appetite and is good color for illnesses of the colon and digestion. ORANGE connects us to our emotional self. Orange as the sacral Chakra means: I FEEL.*

- *YELLOW represents intelligence. YELLOW corresponds to the 3rd Chakra (solar plexus). This is where our UNI (inner self) resides. YELLOW energizes, relieves depression, improves memory, stimulates appetite and helps with digestive disorders. Spiritually YELLOW connects us to our mental self and wisdom. Yellow as the inner self means: I DO.*

- *GREEN manifests healing. GREEN affects the 4th Chakra (heart). GREEN is calming and helps balance our nervous system. GREEN is soothing, relaxing mentally and physically, alleviates depression, anxiety and nervousness. GREEN is a great color for cardiac conditions, high blood pressure, ulcers just to name a few. GREEN also equals growth so should be avoided in cancers or tumors. GREEN is the spiritual color of healing and connects us to perfect love. Green as the heart Chakra means: I LOVE.*

- *BLUE is the color of health. BLUE affects the 5th Chakra (throat). BLUE is a good color for respiratory illness or throat infections. BLUE is calming, cooling and a good color to counteract hypertension. BLUE spiritually connects us to health and holistic thought. Blue as the throat Chakra means: I SPEAK MY TRUTH.*

- *INDIGO represents intuition. INDIGO affects the 6th Chakra (brow or third eye). INDIGO is a good color to use for sinusitis, immunity or lack thereof, and any skin problems. Too much INDIGO can cause depression. INDIGO connects us spiritually to our superconscious. Indigo as the third eye or brow Chakra means: I SEE.*

- *VIOLET brings us faith. VIOLET affects the 7th Chakra (Crown) which is our connection to all things spiritual. VIOLET can be cleansing, strengthening, awakening, suppresses appetite, provides a peaceful environment. VIOLET affects the skeletal system of the body and can be good for arthritis, cancerous conditions and improvement of immune system. Excellent for headaches, migraines and purifying to the system. VIOLET connects us to our spiritual selves. Violet as the Crown Chakra means: I UNDERSTAND.*

- ***BLACK – Feminine***

- ***WHITE – Masculine***

- ***GOLD – Masculine***

- ***SILVER – Feminine.***

An example of working with color could be the clothing you choose, the crystals you use or the colors you paint your home. Your Reiki space should be painted a color that helps you to feel grounded, at peace and one that is pleasing to you and your Clients. I originally started out with a Coral (combination of red, orange and yellow) Reiki room. I wanted the room to be warm and welcoming to my Clients. I have since changed my space and it is now a silvery neutral color. I have added pictures, crystals, blankets etc. in other colors that I wish to utilize for my treatment space. Whatever colors you choose know that they will be right for you and your work.

Color becomes another element of our formula especially when using Crystals that directly affect the energies of the Chakras. I just love color. They "speak" to you on an emotional and vibrational level similar to that of Crystals.

DOWSING
(Use chart on page 94)

The next part of my class covers Dowsing. I give each student a pendulum with their packet, explain what it is, how it works and I also give them a chart. I have to say Dowsing is fun to learn, has many applications. Dowsing is a vital tool and the foundation of my diagnostic process. Using this tool allows the practitioner to gain instant knowledge as to the facts of the state of the Etheric body and the Chakra system. Yes, the physical body manifests symptoms outwardly however they have begun quite some time ago in the Etheric or Shadow body. So, considering this part of my diagnosis helps me to know if the energy is flowing, the spin of the Chakra is open fully and it is at this level I can connect intuitively and get information also. I can ask questions here, I can place imagery in the Chakra or simply ask that the spin open more fully which allows the energies that all the body needs to function at an optimal level.

We begin working with the Yes and No. Use the pendulum and program the YES/NO. Once each student feels comfortable with this by practicing; we will use it further to learn how to diagnose the Chakras and we can also ask questions if needed. I also recommend the book "Letter to Robin" from American Society of Dowsers if you have a further interest in learning more detailed information or take a class. The American society of Dowsers offer ongoing classes and most likely in your area. If you don't own a pendulum –you can simply make one using a threaded needle or a shortened chain of some sort with a stone or pendant on the end. Don't get too focused on the pendulum itself. It is only a tool to use. I have many of them. You can buy them online or in stores that carry metaphysical items. There are some nice ones that have a shaped crystal at the end and it is nice to have one designed specifically for that use especially if you will be using this tool all the time. In my class, part of the package includes a pendulum.

I am a Dowser and I call myself specifically a Healing Dowser/Space Clearer. Dowsing as you may or may not know has been used throughout the centuries to find water, lost objects, and remove negative energies called "Space clearing". To program and learn how to use the pendulum we begin with the simplified chart I have included. Get used to the feel of the pendulum and hold it in your hand so you can connect with it energetically. Hold it loosely but not so it will drop out of your fingers. I hold mine about ¾ of the way up on the chain and you can begin to program it by using your chart. Start with Yes and swing it gently up and down until you feel comfortable with that movement saying the Yes in your mind. Then start the pendulum gently spinning and ask a question that you know is a Yes and ask it. Most of my students are amazed when the pendulum answers with a Yes.

Do the same for the No and keep practicing until you are entirely comfortable with these movements. That is all there is to it for now unless you decide to delve further into Dowsing. You can get really detailed with your questions if you wish but most Dowsers I know just use the Yes and No and really once you have used the pendulum for a long time you don't even need it anymore after a while but that is another story. Never ask a question that you do not want an answer to! If you ask "Am I going to die?" the pendulum is going to answer "Yes" because we are all going to die at some time or another. It cannot answer when. The pendulum can only answer Yes or No. Use your common sense. Approach the usage as an inherent part of your formula.

How do we use the pendulum as a diagnostic tool? When the client is on the table or in the massage chair, starting at the Crown Chakra I will place the pendulum over that area a few inches above them, gently start it spinning and ask, "Is this Chakra open?" the pendulum will answer spinning either a 'Yes' or 'No' answer.

If it is a 'Yes', I will say "Show me the spin" and the pendulum will spin either clockwise or counter clockwise. I have found most people are clockwise in direction although I am counter clockwise. Is this a surprise? Usually but not always all Chakras spin in the same direction although I have seen clients with different directions for different Chakras.

I have no reason why at this time for either direction. Assuming the answer was 'Yes' and the spin is clockwise and it seems to be spinning fairly well I may move on. Note here: sometimes the spin may be tight and small, if so I may ask "May we open the spin wider?" and the pendulum will open up a wider spin. Why do I do this? Remembering that the energy is flowing through the Chakra and that is why I am dowsing to begin with, we are asking to open the spin to facilitate a more readily available amount of energy which to my mind is healthier for the energy body. Now what happens if the pendulum has answered 'No'? I then would ask "Do I have permission to open this Chakra?" the pendulum will answer either 'Yes' or 'No' and then I would ask again "Show me the spin" and depending on that answer we would continue from there. In reality I have never had a 'No' when asking for this permission because the client has really already given me permission to work on them by coming to me in the first place. However, it still comes under that heading of never assume, so I always ask permission. Depending on the Chakra that needed this work we need to discern what the Client may need to work on. A common example would be the throat Chakra not being open. This would mean that person is not speaking their own truth, and this seems to be the case with a lot of women. They are inhibited for whatever the reason. By opening this spin, placing crystals, doing the Reiki hopefully this person will learn to speak their truth without being hurtful. It all goes back to way of thinking. So, I would continue down from the Crown Chakra to the Root Chakra in this manner until I was satisfied that each Chakra was flowing correctly. I may at that time place my hands on the feet to check the Chakras there to feel if the energy feels as if it is flowing.

Note here: All of this is done in my mind as far as asking the questions while physically using the pendulum, however if you are new to this you probably will do this out loud for a time until you are comfortable with all the modalities.

Ok so I have made my initial diagnosis and beginning treatment with the Dowsing of the Chakras and opening or widening any that seemed not to be flowing correctly. What does energy "feel" like? I feel it as a tingly feeling in my hands and sometimes a warmth or coolness depending on the person. Each student has to develop this skill through practice and by deliberately tuning in and using their own intuition. Some students have felt it immediately while others may have to work at it. Trust yourself and you will get it. Taking Reiki 1 should allow you to feel something in your hand Chakras. Once you have been Attuned you may be amazed at what you are feeling.

My next step would be to scan (Auric) the body with my hands to get a "feel" for any hot or cold spots or intuitive impressions of dis-ease. I start at the head or Crown and scan down the right side (I am right handed) if you are so inclined you may start at the left. I go slowly, and I try to "tune-in" to that person. My hands are directly in their AURA. So hopefully if there is any information there I may be able to pick up on it. This is something that some people have as a natural gift and some people need to learn. At times you may just feel something as a slight indication of heat or coolness so once I have scanned both sides and perhaps down the center I might ask the client as an example "I felt something at the hip area – are you experiencing hip pain or pain in your lower back?" They may say yes or no. We go on from there and I make a mental note to do some extra Reiki work in that area no matter what answer I may get from the Client. Another example might be that I suggest if they haven't noticed anything would be that they get it checked out by their Dr. whatever it may be as sometimes there is an issue that has gone undetected and this can be an early warning sign. Remember you can only suggest. Also, do not unduly alarm them just suggest a follow up so then it is up to them if they wish to do so. I only do this if my intuition is strongly telling me there is a problem. You also may have certain Clients that come frequently. I have found in this case that once you "know" them you may not have to do a scan as you may already know the issues. Remaining open and fluid in your approach will allow you the discernment to pass on this particular part of the treatment. I have frequently been "tested" so to speak by Clients who do not mention some issues just to see if you will pick up on it. Once they know and trust you that issue should resolve itself unless it is a cancer or chronic disease. As a new practitioner you may want to mention the fact that you are inexperienced and would appreciate any input before and after the treatment. This will help you with your formula long-term and since you will be using all your symbols you will hopefully be covering everything that is needed. Also, Reiki knows where to go and what to do. The Teams also help with the treatment so don't get bogged down if you "forget" something. They do step in and work along with you.

Everyone has intuition or "gut feeling". Most of us have not developed this innate tool. Begin by just "listening" to your gut which in Huna is your body-mind or your Uni. Your body-mind is connected to everything. Therefore, if you are open and trust it you can get information that may help you in any given situation, not just when using Reiki.

Going back to the scan, I also place my hands on the feet because as we noted earlier there are Chakras on the bottom of the foot and I can feel if the energy is flowing. To me it feels like a tingling feeling. This comes under the heading of intuition or opening the 3rd eye. Please do not get intimidated. As you work with these energies these things should come to you. Whatever happens is right for you. I then also check the hand Chakras to see if that energy is flowing correctly. I am all about getting as much information as possible. Just remember that we are trying to get the energy flowing through the body so however you can imagine it will be fine. Visualization does not always come easily to people so just trust yourself if it doesn't. Just "know" that whatever you are doing is working as it should be.

An exercise for those very beginners who want to learn to visualize might be to look at an object and it can be as simple as looking at or focusing on your hand. Really look at it and notice all the details, how long are the fingers, what color is the skin, what is the shape of the fingers etc. Then close your eyes and try to picture the object or your hand or whatever you have decided to try to visualize. At first you may not see it in your minds eye. However you do "know" what it looks like. Keep working on it until you have a clear picture (when you close your eyes) in your minds eye of that object whatever it may be. Once you have done this with one object you will be able to do it with others when you really pay attention and notice the details. Keep working on it. To some people it comes as easily as breathing to others it takes concentrated effort. A very few never are able to do this. If that is the case then just trust that the energy is there and as I said before however you do the work will be right for you at that time. You DO know what it looks like. Trust yourself!

Never compare yourself to others is a mantra of mine! I see many of those newly on their path who get intimidated by those of us who may have been called much sooner. We are all called in different ways. The Universe is wondrous and diverse and so should we be! You are perfect as you are NOW. You are where you are supposed to be right NOW. Yes, we may know the same modalities and perhaps practice them in similar fashion however we all have our own life experience, past life experience and different Angels and Guides who work with us to express our Vision & Gifts on this plane of existence. We should never be in competition with each other as Alchemical Reiki Light Workers. We are here to serve to the best of our ability. We are here to love & help each other to the best of our ability. Honor differences. Really become part of the team.

I know I keep talking about intuition and some of you may think you are not and never will be intuitive. Not so. We all have intuition. Some of us just need to work at developing it. It all comes down to trust. Trust yourself, trust your gut. Your intuition comes from your subconscious mind or your Uni. Your subconscious mind resides in your solar plexus Chakra area or your gut. We are all connected. We have all the information available to us if we can get out of our own heads and allow the subconscious mind the freedom to expand. This is a retraining of your thinking also. It will come. Reiki changes the way you think of yourself and others once you have taken in the information, have the attunements and begin to work with it. You begin to open up the third eye and see things in new ways. Intuition begins to come to you. Allow it to happen. Your sincere desire to learn this modality and other modalities to help yourself and others will begin opening this door for you. As your real spirituality grows your intuition will grow along with it. You may look back and realize that you had it all along. In HUNA your subconscious mind is comparable to a 7-year-old child – very literal and has charge of your memories and all the bodily processes. Your subconscious mind can also connect to all other minds in the Universe and get information. Some people are born with this GIFT and others can train themselves to grow it so to speak. The seed is there in all of us. That is why I say to be careful what you say to yourself by not owning anything that you do not want to become literal to you. We are also a reflection of our environment and the "tapes" that we have been programmed with as children hence our minds creating dis-ease. Our entire way of thinking needs to change in order to become what we were truly created to be. I know this is probably the most monumental task you will ever undertake. You will continue to work on this Alchemical formula for yourself for the rest of your life.

When you use Reiki and it is channeling through your hands or body you are also receiving it! What a blessing for all concerned. Reiki also helps open you to your gifts of intuition and whatever else you may be attracted to. Also, remember that this is not your stuff! Meaning do not take on the Clients' burdens. I would suggest surrounding yourself with Light that allows nothing to enter except Love.

Ok so you have spoken to your client, Dowsed the Chakras, and scanned the Aura. So now what? Now, I would place crystals on and around the Clients' body. A good place for a beginner to start is to look at the Chakra chart noticing that the Chakras are the color of the rainbow. A good basic rule of thumb here is use the same color crystal for the same color chakra. As you work with and learn more about Crystals you can expand. Also, if you are intuitive or you know the properties you can also use that as a guideline. There are many good books out there and some of my favorites are by Philip Permutter. He calls crystals the Stone People and crystals have their own vibration and their work is subtle. I do know they also have a consciousness that we can directly work with and tap into. Once you begin to accumulate the ones you are "attracted" to you can meditate with them and they will show you what they can do. I also have known Alchemical Light Workers who use lots of crystals using designs and patterns on the body because the vibration is subtle and I am not sure if they are intuitively guided by energy meridians or how that works I just know that it does! If you are looking for a huge enhancement all these things can help and at the very least it is beautiful work. Crystals enhance Reiki or energy work and the ones I am finding most effective so far and that I always use are: Apophyllite, diamonds, Herkimer diamonds and quartz to enhance the Reiki. I put them under, around the table and on or near the client. I also use many crystals that I intuitively choose for each client on each Chakra. We will talk about a symbol later called the Antakharana in another book for the Advanced class. That symbol is also an enhancement to the Reiki. I usually give my clients a Crystal prescription too that they can use to help whatever it may be that they are working on. If I have extra crystals I will give them or suggest they buy them if I do not have them available. I have Crystals all over my home and on my person at all times. Besides being beautiful I just love having them around and having them working for me all the time. You can also make elixirs from certain crystals however be careful and do your research first – you certainly do not want to poison anyone including yourself! I teach another class for those who want to learn more about Crystals and how to work with them to heal the Chakras. Surprisingly, you probably already own some crystals in some of the jewelry you wear. Also, once you become the proud owner of said Crystals do not forget to cleanse them frequently especially if using with clients. I cleanse all the Crystals in my home around the New Year as a rule of thumb. Throughout the year I also cleanse them. You can use Reiki to cleanse them and/or immerse them in salt water. There are also other ways to cleanse the crystals. These also can become a lifetime study. I know that everywhere I go some of the "Stone people" want to come home with me. How exciting is that?

I have gentle Music playing usually something New Age (whales, flute, ocean etc.) and if the person is not allergic I may spray a de-stress spray or use an essential oil spray for de stressing. Let me say that Music is how the Angels communicate on the other side. Be guided by your intuition when choosing what will be playing while your Client is with you. Subliminally Music relieves stress also if it is something that a person can connect with. Music just makes the entire experience so lovely and relaxing! This could be considered Sound Therapy. I also have a Tibetan bowl that I may use to help me cleanse my room or home. The bowl can energetically through vibration bring all other vibrations into alignment. Most of the time I am guided to choose Music that each person connects with. I am always amazed that I seem to choose the right Music for my Client.

Utilizing pillows and coverings helps me make my client as comfortable as possible. Many of my clients end up falling asleep and you know what? That is fine and as long as I don't have another appointment scheduled right away I leave them to it. Obviously they need it and the treatment has worked on some level for de-stressing.

As an RMT I have six symbols plus two that came to me in a meditation to use. In the Reiki I and II classes you will get three symbols. I normally do these to cleanse my space and then again once the client is lying down with their eyes closed. In the first class you will only be using the energy and learning how to do a treatment. I also have two extra symbols which appeared to me in a dream that are used for specific diseases. Those I will share in the final book and in my Master Classes.

Once the client is comfy I will put a tissue over the eyes however not covering the nose as we want to make sure they do not feel suffocated in any way. Please look at the chart. Working on the head for the longest time is the most important because it sets the tone and the relaxation for the rest of the treatment. Your client will go into a meditative state. Be cognizant and ask at the beginning if the client has any issues with turning over. You may find with abuse or back pain or other issues that persons will feel too vulnerable lying on their stomachs. Be mindful at all times and guided by your clients needs. You can do a completely effective treatment just on the front or with client lying on their side or sitting or however it is comfortable for them. Be flexible. The treatment is all about your clients needs not yours. I will start on either side of the nose, lightly for approximately 1-3 minutes, gently sliding hands down to in front of the ears 1-3, then I will come up slightly forward of the crown 1-3, down on shoulders 1-3, neck but not too close 1-3 and by this time, your client should really be completely relaxed and in their own space. Normally, I do not talk unless the client does or I receive a "guidance" for them. However, if the client is really in need I may do a sort of meditative hypno–trance type guidance whereby we are asking their Angel or Guide to help them with a particular issue they may have indicated they needed help with at the beginning when we did the intake. I diverge here with my method from most traditional Reiki practitioners in that I do not like to lift the head to place hands underneath unless the Client has migraine or headache issues as I feel it interrupts the meditative state. If the Client is able to turn over, we can work on the back of the head at that time. I also find that it makes the newly initiated Reiki person nervous as to when and how to do so. The newbie gets caught up in worrying about it and it detracts from the entire experience for all concerned. Remember hand placements are a guidance and Reiki flows where it will. So as I said, to facilitate a completely relaxing experience I choose not to lift the head to place my hands under it. You may choose to do something different as part of your formula.

Every session I have ever done has been unique and wonderful. I am guided completely by my intuition and what I am getting from the client. Then I will move to the body and begin working. Now, when I previously "scanned" I may have made mental notes as to places I wanted to work on specifically and I may go to those places first and place my hands on those areas. I may even do the symbols again on those areas specifically. Note: Remembering that we cannot direct Reiki we do our best however, the Reiki goes where it will and does what it does. We cannot always see or know what levels it is working on or even when it is working. For example: I once had a client who had back issues come to me with the unrealistic expectation that they would be completely healed instantaneously on my table! I told them- if I could do that I would be on Television with possibly Oprah or Dr. Oz! I felt badly that they had this unrealistic expectation. To make a long story short, I did hear later that person did decide to lose the weight they needed to lose, worked out to strengthen those back muscles and over all improved what they needed to make their back better. I was disappointed at the time that the client felt unhappy with my work, however I did feel that the Reiki ultimately worked on other levels. So we never know how, where or when it may work just know that it will. I do know that normally when we lay our hands on, it does usually provide some sort of relief immediately or soon thereafter although as previously noted that is not always the case. This was also a much-needed lesson for me because at this point I thought that I was this magical "healer" and could do anything! Would that I could! My sincere desire to help people is what motivates me, and it was a blow to my ego. There should be no ego involved. This work is not about us personally. When we do Reiki, we are a channel; similar to the same way a pipe is for water. Unfortunately, there is nothing magical about that. Moreover, we seem to "draw" those clients to us whom we resonate with or are familiar with. Meaning we are familiar with their issues or we need to learn a lesson from them. So, a person who feels as if they are "carrying the weight of the world" may evidence it by back or shoulder pain. See what I mean? Does it make sense to you?

Another philosophy I live by is that we get back what we put forth. I use blessing and gratitude in order to receive the same in abundance. Your perception or how you view your world is another HUNA thought: the world is what you think it is. If you can get your mind retrained and help your clients to retrain their thinking (however remembering you are not their Mother or God) these newer healthier thoughts also will help them release dis-ease. A note here also: I keep mentioning HUNA which is a Hawaiian philosophy which I live by and incorporate into everything. If you would like more information about it you can look it up – there are many great books out there. The ones I would highly recommend is *HUNA* and *Urban Shaman* by Serge Kahili King and *Bowl of Light* by Hank Wesselman. At the end of the session I sometimes give the client an affirmation to work with. Affirmations place positive thoughts into our subconscious mind redirecting us to newer healthier ways of thinking. I use them every day, so you see we are all always working on something. Every one of us no matter where we are on our path needs to be working on something because we are Human! How exciting really because we get to learn new things all the time, meet new people and gain new blessings by sharing all these gifts.

Continuing on- we are working on the body. Look at the chart. Be mindful of body parts however, don't be too afraid or caught up in it. One of the reasons I place a sheet or light blanket over the person is that it sort of de-sexes them. They feel comfortable in any weather and you can just think about Reiki. The next traditional placement is under the left breast both hands together 1-3 minutes, then moving or sliding under right breast 1-3 making sure not to touch the breasts as you do not want the client to become uncomfortable with you, then left hip 1-3, right hip 1-3, then right shoulder-left hip (ping-pong), left shoulder-right hip, right hip-left knee, left hip-right knee, right hip-right knee, right knee-foot, left hip-left knee, left knee-left foot, and finally hands on both feet to feel flow. You should also do the arms and hands as you never know if the client may have tendonitis or carpal tunnel or any variety of issues. The arms have a tendency to be overlooked for some reason. There are of course Chakras in the palms which can also be checked for flow. This is also where the Reiki symbols will be placed at the time of Attunement. Since this is where you will "feel" Reiki, I think it is absolutely vital to do some work here on the client also. At this point you will ask client to turn over if they have indicated they wanted to in the beginning.

Prior to talking about the back let's discuss what I heard called "ping pong" energy. Remembering that Reiki is all about getting energy flowing throughout the Chakras, I am and you are training yourself to feel and "see" the energy flowing, however that looks to you or feels to you. The way I feel it is a tingling feeling and I visualize it like water flowing. So when you are working on opening up the energy for example from hip to opposite knee what comes to my mind is something like the old Atari game ping pong visualizing the little ball bouncing back and forth between the paddles. So, you want the energy to bounce back and forth to open up the flow. You can practice by placing your hands on someone's hip and opposite knee and closing your eyes, tuning in and picturing this little ball of energy bouncing back and forth between them. What you get may startle you. In the beginning it may be slow and pick up speed as the channel opens up. I feel that it helps open the flow and release any blockages that we may not have felt while we were scanning. The scanning is called Auric scanning just to reiterate remembering that repetition breeds remembering. It gives you interactive feedback in your own mind of what you are doing. You're trying to "sense" the energy yourself passively and this is just one way you may be able to do so. It helps you to feel what you are doing rather than standing there pretending or floundering or hoping that it is working. Trust yourself- it will come and if some other image comes to your mind be open and you will get it. This is what particularly works for me. We all have blockages, so this ping-pong energy is just one method to visualize energy to help facilitate breaking up the blockage.

The client has agreed to turn over, so you help them do this and position them comfortably, removing or placing pillows as needed and placing a sheet or blanket over them again. I have an Earthlite table which I would highly recommend. It may seem rather expensive however it is very sturdy, easy to clean and able to hold up to 500 pounds, and you can carry it out to client's homes or use it however you wish. Getting back to the treatment, you can begin by placing hands at shoulder level (not covering the spine) 1-3 minute, right hand on right shoulder, then sliding right hand to left shoulder blade as you practice it becomes a smooth flowing motion and look at the chart while you are practicing. Also, once you have learned Reiki and been attuned you can keep a chart of the symbols in front of you until you are comfortable with them. I insist on committing the symbols to memory though as you will find yourself wanting to do a lot of your work in your mind later on also called Remote or distance work. Then the hands go to waist level then together at the coccyx bone. Once these four positions are done sweep the aura once on each side and down the center. I use a large Selenite wand to do this however, you can just use your hands. This helps clear any residual negativity and flick the fingers thereby flicking away any toxic energies. The client may be sleeping and use your judgment whether to allow them to continue or lightly touch their shoulder and help them up. Let them sit for a little while to "come back to earth". Give them some water and I again highly recommend the client to drink plenty of water to remove any toxicity that may have been generated from the energies being stirred up. At this point, you can offer another treatment or ask the client to get back in touch it is up to you and your discernment as each situation is different. If the client enjoyed their session a referral recommending you to their friends and family would be appreciated. Some business cards or brochures to hand out if you are doing it as a business along with their crystal prescription, their affirmation and any other information they may have asked for or I feel that may be of interest to them can be given at this time depending entirely on what modalities you have chosen to enhance the Reiki energies.

So, there you have done a "treatment". How do you feel? How does the person you have just worked on feel? What did you notice? You can make some notes when you practice on yourself, friends, family which will allow you to develop your alchemical formula. Notice if your hands feel cold, hot, tingly etc. Ask if they notice anything and if there's anything they would like to share? Make notes if it helps you to do so. I recommend journaling about your experiences as it will help you to grow into your Reiki and also on your other paths of learning. Many times my Clients receive images and ideas while on the table. This is because you have gotten them into a meditative state and they are open to receiving from their "team".

At Level 1 in Reiki you do not get a symbol. You learn about the energy, the Chakra system and pendulum dowsing, crystals, sound therapy, sometimes color usage in my classes. We all try a treatment. When I sit down to do a class I also use Doreen Virtue's Angel cards to start out after each person has introduced themselves and given a short synopsis of why they are taking Reiki. These cards are always positive and when we talk about the "message" and what it means to the person. I usually get some intuition and guidance about where they may be on their own particular "path". Usually the classes are pretty consistent in that the students are pretty close in knowledge and openness. We usually take the entire day for Level 1 which is not as much time as I would like to devote to it however our lives are hectic so this has to suffice. At the end of this first day each student is Attuned separately. I do not prefer group Attunements and most RMT's do not do them to my knowledge. I try to do things individually if at all possible. My classes are usually small and personal. Most of my students remain my friends once we have met. We usually do the Tree® grounding meditation and during one of the days we participate in a Guardian Angel Guide mediation. I really like to save Reiki Guides for Level III. I require anyone going beyond Level I and II to student teach with me to attain Level III and RMT. At Level II the students get three symbols and that day they then get Attuned for those three symbols which allow them to do just about anything you can imagine or think of. Most students are fulfilled taking Reiki I & II. They are Attuned at least twice and get three symbols to work with that allow them to do an amazing amount of energy work that continues to grow as the student studies and works with it. Many other modalities can be incorporated into your usage of Reiki at these levels. I find that once this door is open many other paths open up also. You will find what works for you and with you as you grow into the role of Alchemical Light Worker. Do I mean those words implying someone like a superhero-type figure? I simply mean someone who chooses to do good however that gift manifests for them. It can be as simple as working on being a better person. We never know how or why we bring Light sometimes or even that we have. We can only choose to do the best we can with what we have at each given moment. If we fall down, then we just have to pick ourselves back up and move along. We have come to this physical plane to learn with help of our spiritual consciousness which Reiki and the other "tools" help to awaken and heal to a certain degree also. My belief is that we are never really completely perfect until we return Home from whence we came. Reiki energy is a gift from Home or the Source to use here as we are able.

I am sure by now you are wondering what the heck is an Attunement? The Reiki Attunement is a sacred ritual whereby the symbol or symbols are placed into your hand and Crown Chakras and your Aura forever allowing you to "call" them and "use" their energy. The student is not allowed to know the ritual until it is explained just prior to the Attunement. Some of it may seem rather strange or seem silly to you however, go along and it is rather brief perhaps taking all of ten minutes or so. The "ritual" goes back to the Usui teaching which I am sure was based in part on his knowledge of Buddhist ritualism. So, he may have created this ritual from those beliefs. The subconscious mind absolutely loves ritual! It places a spiritual significance upon whatever it is you are partaking of. Think about religious ceremonies. Those ceremonies are comprised of rituals that have been handed down through generations. Do know that once you "have" Reiki it does change you on some subliminal and energetic level. Your third eye opens, and your perception of the world is enhanced. I found on each level that as I progressed new levels of intuition opened for me and new Mentors along with Guides & Angels came to work with me. There are also healing Attunements which the RMT can use to sort of "power up" the treatment and can be particularly effective for those patients who may have a severe or chronic illness such as cancer or something of that magnitude. Reiki can also be used to assist those who are "crossing over" to make that transition easier. You can "send" Reiki to assuage grief of loved ones to assist at the time of dying and after too. Also, when you go to Reiki shares a lot of the RMT's will give Attunements *again* which allows the energy to flow even better. I know that the more you use it the stronger it becomes likening it to working out your muscles. You know you have to be consistent in order to keep them in shape.

I firmly believe that each Reiki person should get re-attuned as many times as possible as it helps strengthen the energy opening the synapses and creating new ones.

ATTUNEMENTS

(Reiju)

The Dictionary describes the word ***Attunement*** like this: "to bring into harmonious or responsive relationship; a feeling of being as one with". The RMT utilizing a ritual (which has been passed down and I am assuming because Dr. Usui was a monk taken from that tradition) physically places the symbols into the crown Chakra and the hand Chakras by drawing them and calling them in their mind. The ritual can be subject to some variation depending on the RMT. They may add enhancements that include: music, crystals, incense or make it brief, again it is all up to personal choice as to the peripherals of the ritual. The basic ritual remains regarding how the symbols are placed into the AURA, CHAKRAS etc. In HUNA once we come to know someone we become connected to them through something called the AKA which is like an invisible cord if you will; so by accepting this ritual you are becoming connected to your RMT and the Reiki energy and the Source where it comes from. The Attunement is an alchemical reiki ritual that connects you to your lineage spiritually.

As I mentioned previously, there are also healing Attunements which the RMT can do for their Clients to "ramp" up the treatment. Frankly, on what basis this all works I haven't a clue except that it comes directly from the Source of all things and everything has a vibration so saying it, drawing it and seeing it all send out a notification of intent. I also know that it works and you will become amazed at how well it does. We are connected spiritually through the Reiju (attunement) to the Source and also to all those we connect to with Reiki. This most likely comes under that heading of we will find out in greater detail when we get to the other side. Since I know and have been shown that I am a healer on the other side I probably already know these things at the subliminal level.

The Attunement begins working with your AURA and opens channels similar to a rivulet of water becoming a small stream and growing over time into a creek, well you get the picture. We are always a work in progress. Whatever you want to become is up to you. I do know that new synapses open in your brain the more you use the energies and the more you get new Attunements the wider these open to allow for more energy. Does this make sense to you?

Once you become Attuned and open yourself to this new energy and new way of thinking and perception of the world- new paths open. Whether you choose them or not is up to you. Reiki will always be there in your Aura even if you do not use it. The energy is always available to you instantly. I only have to think of it and I can feel the tingling in my hand Chakras. How warm or cool, if you will, is that!?

That concludes how I teach and use Reiki Level I and II along with introduction into modalities of: HUNA, Angels, Dowsing, Chakras, Crystals, Intuition just to name a few. This is a lot of information to process. My recommendation is keep rereading this book, use the charts and work with the energy once you have taken your class. Practice as much as you are able. Even as you pass on to more advanced levels it is always good to come back to your foundations as there are things that can be forgotten or just need refreshing. You will always learn something new! These foundations form the basis for your own personal Alchemy and are what has set you on your path to becoming an Alchemical Reiki Light Worker!

REIKI II

Having taken Reiki I of course you want to continue on to Level II. Many students take I and II in a weekend. When you learn it this way you really are only skimming the surface of the waters. You do get a good basic grounding in the energy and symbols however, if you as the student do not make the commitment to work diligently with the information you really do lose a chance to open the door to a new world. Do I mean you have to drop everything else? You work it into your life as you are able and inclined to. Some feel called to do it occasionally as a gift to themselves, their pets, family and friends. Reiki also works on inanimate objects and situations. Others may feel challenged to create new businesses although I will say that preferably you will be an RMT if you do decide to pursue that path. It all depends on each individual. Do whatever is right for you. You may learn Reiki now, learn other modalities as you go along and later on changes may allow you to do this on a more ongoing basis. It is all up to you, your path and your gifts. A suggestion I would make to you is this: Use the energy at least once per day even if it is in your mind. Perhaps an easy start would be to send Reiki to a list of your family members and as you move along your path you can decide how else you will apply this gift in your life. Even devoting ten minutes a day will help you open to this work. I am absolutely sure you are and will become an amazing Reiki practitioner!

During Reiki II you get three symbols that come from the foundation of Reiki by Dr. Usui. You learn each one by seeing, saying and drawing it over and over again. It may sound tedious however we learn through repetition. I also have a large chart out once the symbols have been shown so the students can see them and use them throughout the day. We also review the material from the previous class. We all get on the table and take turns giving and receiving a treatment. This class focuses on sending the student out there with the ability to give a full-fledged Reiki treatment from start to finish. We need the practice with symbols because we aren't familiar with the Japanese language firstly. Secondly, the symbols are Japanese Kanji or letters or some combination thereof. Thirdly but not least, we would remain at Level 1 if we did not have the symbols etched forever in our minds. We need to be able to draw them instantly however we are called to do so.

As I said in the book one, the first three Reiki symbols are based on Japanese script or words. I myself do not know the Japanese language however, each symbol has a meaning. I do know that when you "draw' the symbol with your hand, finger, with a pen or in your mind energy is ramped up and you can feel a difference. How this happens is a mystery to some but again, I would venture that it is the vibration that signals to the energy. Quantum Physics say that each experiment is affected by the person performing it. The person performing the experiment puts their energy, intention and hope for an outcome thus affecting that outcome. So it would follow in my thinking knowing this, that the person who comes for the treatment with their intention and hope and so too, the Practitioner uses their intention, hope and skills thus creating an alchemical outcome. Reiki comes from the Source of all things is what I have been told and believe so the symbols are like power words is the best way I can describe it or perhaps to the computer generation it is like using the CAPS LOCK key for the energy is the best analogy I can make. This becomes a new Mantra: See, Say, Draw…. We must always have intention if we are working in our minds or working with our hands.

CHO-KU-REI

The first symbol we will be learning is called CHO-KU-REI (cho-ku-ray). This is known as the power symbol with the meaning being "by Imperial Decree". As you may or may not know the Japanese were living in a Monarchy and their Emperor was considered to be a God and whatever he said or did became the Imperial decree or law. This symbol is a command to connect to the Source or law of the Universe . Think of it as turning on the switch for energy. When I use this in my mind I see a swirling spiral of energy focused on whatever it is I am working on at that time. In your beginning studies I would recommend using the symbols in the order you learned about them. If you decided to continue on to RMT you may change the order in which you use them. You will draw this symbol, see it and say it out loud as many times as needed to fully memorize it as you will do with all the symbols. You cannot be as effective if you do not memorize these symbols. You may keep a sheet of them drawn and named for reference however to really progress on this path you need the memorization. I cannot stress this enough. You really should not receive Certification if you cannot "call" the symbols properly. In my classes I require the student to show me the symbols in their entirety meaning they need to say it and draw it for me with paper, in air and in their mind.

This allows me to see where we may need further work although I truly cannot see into their minds~and wouldn't really want to.

CHO KU REI can be used to clear negativity. You can place that symbol over your home, car or person for protection and you can "sandwich" whatever you are working on to ramp it up. Sandwiching means to use the symbol first and last containing the other symbols inside like a sandwich filling. You can also draw this symbol with each hand at the same time to create a powerful connection a sort of "double" effect. As I said before I use all my symbols for whatever I am working on.

In class we would begin drawing this symbol until we become comfortable with it. I will have it on a chart for viewing and once we have practiced see, say, draw then I will require you to draw it in the air and in your mind. In the last part of the class prior to Attunement and Certification I will want to see you use it on paper and in the air as you would when you do a treatment. Practicing it will build up tactile memory. You should become proficient and able to do this instantly. You will be able to do it, don't have any doubt in yourself! Eventually, the symbol will appear in your mind in its entirety. Even though I can picture the symbols this way unless pressed for time, I will draw it, see and say it. I draw the symbols in my mind frequently as I do not always have the time or am in a place where I cannot physically draw them. The symbols are also an absolutely integral part of your formula. Without them you really do not have a formula. It would be like having H2 without the O...thus no water as a substitute explanation of the Reiki Alchemical formula.

CHO KU REI is a spiral shaped symbol. The spiral shape has been in existence for thousands of years. Many artifacts that have been uncovered have this symbol. I would say this is the easiest to memorize because subconsciously you have already seen similar work and perhaps may even have jewelry or something in your home that is a version of this symbol.

CHO KU REI

This page is intentionally left blank in order that you as the student may practice drawing this symbol as many times as you need to –thereby making it your own.

SEI HEI KI

SEI HEI KI (say-hay-key) is the symbol that means God and man become one. This symbol connects with emotion and our mental processes thus re-aligning ourselves with the Source, whatever you may choose to call it. We are perfect, perhaps not on the physical plane, but in Spirit once we go home. The third eye is a good extra placement for this symbol.

Utilizing this symbol to enhance our mental and emotional well-being also de-stresses our body. We know that stress causes dis-ease. Each symbol also has its own vibration. Your vibration is enhanced by the usage of the three symbols attuning your energy body with the energy from the Source.

We are what we think or how we think. Sei hei ki creates balance between our mental and emotional processes. Using it also helps clear negative energies and thoughts. I sometimes do my symbols then place Sei hei ki in my third eye to help me meditate. If you are like me it becomes difficult to turn off the "monkey brain". You will of course, as you go along your personal path find many other ways in which to add the symbols into your Alchemical formula for Reiki.

This symbol would in Huna represent the Uhane or the conscious mind. It also creates a bridge between the three. Remember I stated before that it is always good to have our three selves in alignment. This symbol can help to achieve that goal for you and your Client.

SEI HEI KI

This page is intentionally left blank in order that you as the student may practice drawing this symbol as many times as you need to –thereby making it your own.

HON SHA ZE SHO NEN

Hon Sha Ze Sho Nen (hone-sha-zay-sho-nen) can seemingly be the most complicated and intimidating of the three symbols.

As a Reiki Practitioner Level 2 this symbol becomes your most creative piece of the Alchemical formula. This symbol allows you to send Reiki to the past, present and future.

Considered the Distance symbol, it eliminates barriers of time, space or thought. For example, Reiki can be sent to a specific time, date, person, place or thing, a situation or problem. As humans we all have experienced some type of negative situation. This symbol allows us to send Reiki to that situation. Will it change it? No, however it can change the emotion.

We can also ask that the pain be taken but the lesson remain. I am always astounded and amazed at the ways in which we can work with these symbols and the energy. Imagine for yourselves what you can do with this ability to transmute time and space! Mind-boggling is the only word I can think of to describe the amazing work you have access to byusing this symbol.

Utilizing this symbol to "send" Reiki is commonly referred to as "remote Reiki or remote healing". Most of the work I do comes under this heading. If you consider the state of the world today there are myriad possibilities to using this energy. An example could be to send to the issues of disease,homelessness, war, heads of government, and of course, any of us could go on and on. There are many ways you can do "remote" work. Your Alchemial formula will evolve as you grow in the Light. Mine is constantly changing as I add or subtract Clients (which if you remember can be a subject other than human). We as Alchemical Reiki Practitioners are all called to do some facet of this work.

As I said previously, what type of work you do, who you do it with or for and how you develop your formula all depends on your knowledge, gifts and perceptions and how much time you are able to devote to the work. Remembering permission is required, you could use a picture of a person (and they may have asked you for this) and do Reiki for them remotely. I always try to hold a picture in my minds' eye of the person(s) I am working on. If you cannot directly ask for the permission, clear your mind and ask if the permission is granted. I find most of the time I will get a yes. You can always choose to send Reiki to the "team" of whomever and ask that the Reiki be dispensed as needed. I often have people pop into my mind to send Reiki to. How or why this happens I don't know so I just add them to my list. If you have a good connection with animals, they at times too request Reiki. Reiki can become a channel allowing you to connect to the animals you wish to work with.

This symbol **Hon Sha Ze Sho Nen** seems to be the most intimidating to students because it is quite long and involved. The way to learn it is to break it down step by step so you will remember it. Practice, practice, practice is your Mantra for all the symbols! I can remember feeling that I would never be able to master it. However here I am many years later and can summon it instantly to mind. By seeing, saying and drawing, you as the Alchemical Reiki Practitioner will be able to do that also. Be confident in your gifts. You are a blessing and are receiving the blessing of Reiki.

The second day of classes is dedicated to learning the symbols and also to giving and receiving a treatment. We all take turns on and off the table. This allows you to have the memory of what it feels like to give and to receive a treatment. You will continue using your symbols throughout the day. You will also get a copy of them written down so you can continue to practice and learn. Do not let that piece of paper become a crutch! It is the most vital component of your Alchemical formula! You do need to memorize those symbols by seeing, saying and drawing in person in the air, on paper and in your mind.

I do recommend you going over your Reiki information packet that you will receive during your class. I often re-read because there's always something you may have forgotten or need to refresh your memory on. New information comes to light time and again in the same information from the beginning. Re-reading can perhaps cause you to consider information in a new light as you deepen your Practice.

HON SHA ZE SHO NEN

This page is intentionally left blank in order that you as the student may practice drawing this symbol as many times as you need to –thereby making it your own.

GUARDIAN ANGELS

We all have Guardian Angels. They have been with us since before our birth. They may be one of the Archangels or another Being of light who has chosen to work with us on this Path here on Earth. Free Will is a gift to humanity therefore we must ask for their help in order to receive it. There have been exceptions to this whereby there was some sort of prior agreement in place from the other side, but it is not in my gift to know how or what type of agreement was made. So, on the second day of classes I lead a meditation with my students to introduce them to their Guardian Angel if they have not already begun working with Beings of Light. At the beginning of the class we also use the Doreen Virtue Angel or Archangel card deck and at that time whatever card is drawn is usually an indication also of an energy that student is able to access for further help. Everyone can access their Angel. The Angels and Archangels are a form of energy that will come to work with us on this plane of existence. We can call on any one of them at any time. These are spirit beings that can work with unlimited numbers of Humanity at any given moment. They offer us a powerful resource and can provide unusual solutions to problems if we do not place any limitations. Our minds can become somewhat limited by the physical although as you grow on your path you will release some of these blockages and be able to use and incorporate new ways of thinking.

To learn more about Angels and other beings of Light, Doreen Virtue has written many books and also designed many card decks. She offers some guidelines and insight into exactly what gifts each individual Angel can solve our problems with. My guardian is Gabriel. Many see this Angel as female in persona however I see Gabriel as a male persona. He inspires me in my writing and when in need, I ask him to help and guide me. Other Angels and Beings bring other qualities or gifts. I send Reiki every single day to these Beings and those they are working with. I call on them frequently often utilizing certain Angels for specific issues. Angels all have a color and they communicate on the other side by singing. I believe this is why Humanity loves music so much! It truly is the language of the Universe.

So now we will do a meditation. I call it 'Let's Meet Our Angel'®. Let us remember for those who are new to meditation that we need to be sitting comfortably, spine straight, eyes closed, breathing deeply and regularly down into our diaphragm and it also helps to train our bodies' physical response to put the thumb and index fingers together as tactile (body memory) indication that it is time to meditate. We can also use the HUNA breathing technique. After using all your symbols, use your SEI HEI KI symbol on your third eye area. Minimizing noise, perhaps darkening the room, having some quiet, spiritual music, incense if wished etc. will allow you to attain the meditative state. You can get as detailed or make it as simple as you wish. We can train ourselves to ignore outside noises too. It just depends on how much time and energy we wish to devote to this practice of meditation also. Ok let us begin: Close your eyes, breathe, relax… feel yourself settling deeply into your seat. Shoulders relaxing, breath going deeply into your lungs and diaphragm. As you continue to breathe you will feel yourself settling down into your seat. Your body will relax and your mind will quiet. Picture a loving, beautiful place that you feel safe and comfortable in. Perhaps it is a lovely garden or a beach near the ocean or a lake. Perhaps it is a path through a sun-dappled forest…feel a soft, warm breeze caressing your cheek, keep breathing… let it go… you are very safe…your body is releasing tension… it is settling into its place… it feels heavier... you can smell the fragrant air… perhaps you hear waves or birds… breathing softly and deeply… Relaxing… you feel warm, safe, comfortable… you feel a warming light and as you relax you will sense a soft, gentle, loving presence… perhaps you see a colorful glow… you will remember that color… You feel yourself bathed in the color… it is very healing and comforting… you turn and look - there you see a Being… it may be male or female or androgynous… you feel safe and loved and happy to finally be meeting your own personal Angel… Bask in the glow of love… you ask the Being "what is your name?" (if you don't already know)… trust what you get – perhaps your

Angel has a message for you or a gift?... you will remember... you will work together for a long time... you have been working together for a long time...

breathe... relax... trust yourself... light surrounds you... What do you see? Your Angel loves you unconditionally and helps you with all you need anytime when you ask. At this time you are feeling loved and peaceful. Now, it is time to say goodbye but you know that you only have to ask and your call will be answered at the speed of light... slowly... breathe... feeling yourself coming back slowly... Becoming aware of your body, the chair, the room... opening your eyes... when you are ready... open your eyes... Remember the name of your Angel, the color- perhaps a message. I always recommend writing this down to refer back to because sometimes especially with a cryptic message things can become clear at a later date. If your Angel has given you a gift and it exists on this plane, I would recommend you purchasing if you don't already own it to use as a reminder and focus. When working with Angels, Guides or Fairies you may be uncomfortable with those terms so you can also think of them as vessels of energy that are available for our use. Remember I said everything is energy, so you can break it down to that level if you wish. I prefer to be intimately acquainted and work closely with these beings of Light. Also, not everyone works with Archangels. I have many friends who work with Beings that are on that level however you would not recognize their name. We are all gifted to work with Beings that are perfect for our needs. Beings, spirit-guides can come and go. I find myself working with many beings at any given time. If you allow yourself to be open to this new way of utilizing Spirit this will happen for you also.

This page used to write Angel Name, Color & Message:

A complete Reiki treatment

1. Cleanse area with symbols, tune in, breathe and get everything ready for treatment asking your "Team" and their "Team" to join you and your Client.
2. Sit with Client to ascertain needs and formulate a treatment plan. Have Client sign and understand disclaimer.
3. Explain Reiki and how it is provided.
4. Have Client get on the table, chair and get comfortable assisting with pillows, blankets etc.
5. Draw the symbols over the person.
6. Turn on music, place crystals
7. Diagnose Chakras with pendulum
8. Auric scan
9. Meditation if needed, add more crystals if needed.
10. Starting with head to allow Client to relax
11. Work on arms, shoulder to elbow, elbow to hand
12. Moving to shoulders, then under each breast, continuing to waist.
13. Hips, then placing one hand on hip and other hand crosswise to knee using Ping-pong energy on both sides
14. Hip to knee, knee to foot.
15. Check feet and if Client has indicated problems there place hands over Chakra area, you may need to do some extra work here if you are guided to.
16. Turn over if Client has accepted that and start at shoulders place hand on each side of spine left, right and then down to mid back left and right again then down to waist area left and right and finally at coccyx area with both hands.
17. Sweep down each side and middle with hands flicking to rid toxicity or using a crystal or wand.
18. Touch person on shoulder, help sit up, offer water, another appointment if needed and/or brochures.

The treatment plan is a guideline for beginners. You may tweak it as you find your own Alchemical Reiki formula. If giving Reiki in other than a dedicated treatment area be flexible and do a treatment or band-aid Reiki as you have determined what is needed. If there is no table available, you can use a bed or a chair. If using a chair have person lay their head on a table with a pillow and work from the back. Above all remember to be flexible.

I do want to mention that doing a treatment also becomes a Ritual for the Practitioner. Personally, it helps me to keep a sequence of steps so that I do not forget anything. Don't get too bogged down in worrying if you did it right or not remembering to be fluid. Our team and theirs step in if we haven't and that knowledge can relieve your stress. It is good for you to know that whatever you are doing will work and is continuing to work.
Obviously, you are an Empathetic Being who comes to learn and help. Honor yourself and your Alchemical Reiki gifts will work and will definitely help others! They will be very

grateful as am I that you will be joining with me to share this work. I am excited that you are on your Path of discovery in becoming an Alchemical Reiki Light Worker! You have a lot to offer and a sincere, loving desire for this work. Keep learning, questioning and growing in the Light! Above all have fun!

Disclaimer Notice

I, the undersigned do completely understand that the Reiki treatment provided by _____ and that I will receive, in no way replaces conventional medical treatment. Reiki provides stress relief only and does not undertake to claim "Healing".

_____

Please print:

Name:_____

Adddress:_____

_____

Phone:_____

Your Name, address and phone can go here along with handing a brochure or business card. I am excited that you are joining all of the Reiki practitioners here on earth! At the very least you will meet many new people and learn how to apply all that you are learning to situations and people in your life. Have fun.

The Dowsing Chart

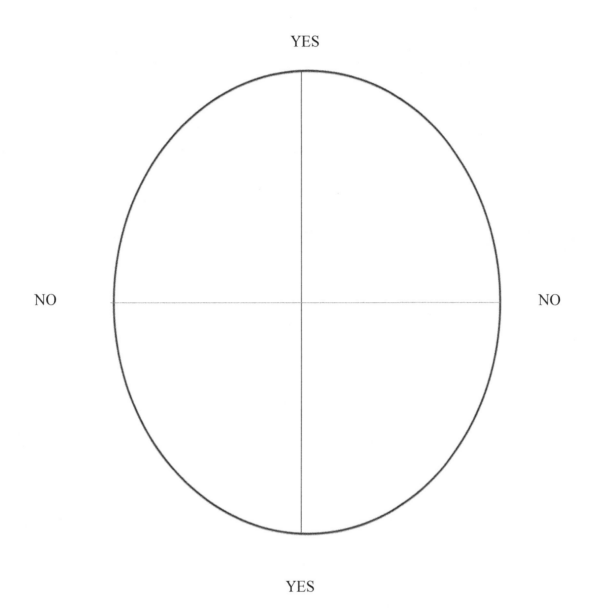

THE REIKI IDEALS

As presented by Mrs. Takata

Just for today, I will let go of anger.

Just for today, I will let go of worry.

Just for today, I will give thanks for my many Blessings.

Just for today, I will do my work honestly.

Just for today, I will be kind to my neighbor and every living thing.